"Christopher Kenworthy doesn't encou... ...on.
With his precise and concise explanati... r
magic, he provides invaluable tutorial... ...
Better still, Kenworthy also gives film '-
mation to help them better appreciate d
emotional responses to the masterwo
— Joe Leydon, writer, *Variety* and MovingP...

"An easy and quick read, *Shoot Like Spielberg* showcases clear examples of ways
to use the camera fluidly within a scene, blending single takes into the illusion of
multiple-camera setups. Revealing these techniques to not be exclusive to those
with big budgets, this book will help you to see the possibilities of using the
camera frame to hide and reveal story to the audience at just the right moments —
all with a single camera and blocking for your actors. A must-read for aspiring
cinematographers and directors."
— Erin Corrado, reviewer, OneMovieOurViews.com

"The ideas, the storytelling, the visuals: Chris Kenworthy knows the master. Chris
also shows how scenes, some classics, some seemingly barely noticed, have made
Spielberg's films endure and transcend."
— Dave Watson, editor, DaveSaysMoviesMatter.com

"In three slim volumes, Christopher Kenworthy has brought a great gift to all film
directors. He has done more than just deconstruct the filmmaking techniques of
three masters; he has also shown us, moment by moment, how the intricate dance
between organic staging and skilled camera technique can elevate what appears to
be a conventional scene into one of cinematic and emotional tension."
— Mark W. Travis, writer, director, author of *Directing Feature Films* and *The Film Director's
Bag of Tricks*

"*Shoot Like Spielberg* intends to encapsulate the 'visual secrets of action,
wonder, and emotional adventure' that any filmmaker can use to capture a bit of
Steven Spielberg's magic. As if it were possible. Surprisingly, author Christopher
Kenworthy comes pretty darn close. And that, in itself, is pretty magical."
— Stefan Blitz, editor-in-chief, Forces of Geek

"Continuing his terrific in-depth look at some of America's finest directors,
Kenworthy turns his discerning eye towards the foremost dream-architect of
American pop culture: Steven Spielberg. There is tremendous craftsmanship in
what some might call Spielberg's unapologetic mainstream spectacle, and it turns
out there's equally commendable craft in Kenworthy's analysis. Here he examines
some of the great Spielberg moments, noting the importance of building tension
through idle conversation that becomes essential in unveiling the lurking evil force
in *Jaws*, or the caffeinated mood and 'waves of tension and release' that ripple
through his giddy comedy *Catch Me If You Can*. The book is like fine wine: You want
to savor it, drink it in, and simply enjoy it. It's a must-have, not just for Spielberg
diehards, but for anyone who considers themselves a true-blue movie fanatic."
— Michael Laskin, author, *The Authentic Actor: The Art and Business of Being Yourself*

"Having the best equipment or raising mounds of money doesn't guarantee your movie is going to be interesting. Making a watchable movie is about how you tell your story. Dialogue is important, but little nuances such as camera moves and actor blocking can turn a boring movie into one that people truly enjoy. Sure, a well-written script is a must, but to bring that script to life, the film must be shot right. Director Steven Spielberg knows how to bring emotion into his films. How can you bring the same emotion into *your* movie? With this book you can. Author Christopher Kenworthy examines scenes from several Spielberg films and teaches you how to incorporate these techniques into your project. For under twenty bucks, you can take home Spielberg's shooting secrets and raise up the storytelling value of your shots. What are you waiting for? Keep this book handy. Store it with your film gear as a constant reference. It will be like Spielberg is hiding in your camera case."

— Forris Day Jr., filmmaker, "Coffee Shop Conversations" entertainment podcast host

"Kenworthy lifts the hood on Spielberg's filmmaking engine and shows us how the high-performance valves and pistons work. *Shoot Like Spielberg* is an essential visual guide for directors and cinematographers who want to learn from moviemaking's master mechanic."

— Todd Klick, author, *Something Startling Happens: The 120 Story Beats Every Writer Needs to Know*

"Call it a book on cinematography or call it a book on film study. Whatever you want to call it, Christopher Kenworthy's book will help you appreciate and understand what Spielberg brings to the screen."

— Matthew Terry, screenwriter, filmmaker, teacher

SHOOT LIKE
SPIELBERG

The Visual Secrets of Action, Wonder, and Emotional Adventure

CHRISTOPHER KENWORTHY

MICHAEL WIESE PRODUCTIONS

Published by Michael Wiese Productions
12400 Ventura Blvd. #1111
Studio City, CA 91604
(818) 379-8799, (818) 986-3408 (FAX)
mw@mwp.com
www.mwp.com

Cover design by Johnny Ink. www.johnnyink.com
Interior design by William Morosi
Copyediting by Ross Plotkin
Printed by McNaughton & Gunn

Manufactured in the United States of America

Library of Congress Cataloging-in-Publication Data

Kenworthy, Christopher.
 Shoot like Spielberg: the visual secrets of action, wonder, and emotional
 adventure / Christopher Kenworthy.
     pages cm
 ISBN 978-1-61593-228-3
1. Spielberg, Steven, 1946--Criticism and interpretation. 2. Motion pictures--
Production and direction. 3. Cinematography. I. Title.
 PN1998.3.S65K47 2015
 791.4302'33092--dc23
                              2015002134

CONTENTS

INTRODUCTION

Stephen Spielberg is a master of visual storytelling, guiding your eye to moments of wonder, surprise, and heartbreak. There are few directors who can tell stories so efficiently, revealing information so precisely while creating intricate scenes of joy, suspense, and horror.

This book shows you why the best moments in his films work so well, and how you can take that knowledge to make your own films work more effectively.

You don't want to copy Spielberg, but you will find that using some of his core techniques makes you a much better filmmaker. You might assume that because he's a big-budget director, you can only achieve these results with lots of equipment. The great beauty of this book is that it shows Spielberg to be one of the most disciplined and inventive directors around, and proves that he can shoot impressive scenes with minimal equipment. With careful placement of actors and a few simple camera moves, he creates scenes that feel like they were shot with ten cameras.

Although Spielberg is incredibly inventive, he uses a number of core techniques to tie his films together, and they are all explained in this book. When I set out to watch his films, I was astonished at how often he would use the same techniques, with a slight variation, to get the right result. This is why the older films, such as *Jaws*, remain relevant. This is also why films such as *Lincoln* are not included in this book. Although *Lincoln* was successful on many levels, it did not introduce any shots or techniques that Spielberg hadn't used before.

Spielberg has shot a lot of films, so choosing the right ones for this book was extremely difficult, but I tried to stick to scenes that could be achieved on a low budget, without CGI, spaceships, aliens, or stunt coordinators. Although Spielberg makes good use of Hollywood's most expensive toys, his greatest skill is his ability to tell a story.

Spielberg can keep a scene active and interesting so that long sequences of dialogue remain fascinating. We get to see entire scenes play out without a single cut. He is also able to tell stories at extreme speed, so when you learn his techniques, you will be able to convey the important parts of your story in an instant.

There is no danger that your films will look like Spielberg films so long as you are telling your own stories. You can take his techniques and apply them to your stories, and you will become a better filmmaker. An understanding of how Spielberg works will open you up to more creative choices when setting up your shots.

Most importantly, you will learn that some of the best camera moves don't require the camera to move at all. Spielberg moves the actors around within a scene with such finesse that it looks effortless. Getting actors to work accurately, hitting such exact marks, can take time — but the results are undeniably brilliant.

Spielberg is often regarded as overly sentimental and childish, but while it is true that many of his films fail in some ways, everything he has shot shows an extraordinary understanding of cinematic language. He makes frequent use of visual contrast and subtle symbolic imagery, giving him far more range than that for which he is often credited. His ability to convey the horrors of war, for example, makes the efforts of many other directors look feeble in comparison.

I hope this book will show you that you can improve your films by directing audience attention throughout a scene, making the most of simple camera moves and careful blocking. When you know how Spielberg creates moments of discovery, fear, and compelling dialogue, you can adapt the ideas to your own style.

When you have finished this book, you will understand how Spielberg approaches a scene, and what he's trying to achieve. You will understand the most efficient ways to get information across, and this will save you time when shooting as well as making your films look better and conveying deeper emotions.

HOW TO USE THIS BOOK

Watch every Spielberg film you can before you read this book, and buy copies of the movies that you can keep, which will allow you to watch these scenes (and others) to decode the techniques. The chapters are filled with spoilers, so make sure you watch the films first. Most of the scenes are from relatively early on in the films to avoid giving too much away, but you should still watch each film before reading the book.

You can work through the book in order, pick a chapter that interests you, or work through according to your favorite films.

The techniques can be applied to your own work. If you're creating a scene that needs Rapid Storytelling, there's a chapter dedicated to such, and you can go straight there. If you want Dynamic Dialogue, you can similarly find the chapter you need.

Before you read the chapter, watch the scene in question if you can, and try to see how and why it works. Then, once you've read the chapter, watch the scene again, perhaps with the sound down so that you can focus on the camera moves and see how the scene has been crafted.

CHAPTER 1

DESPERATE CHASE:

Raiders of the Lost Ark

GOOD CHASE SCENES bring a film to life, and Spielberg is a master of balancing tension, action, and even humor to make a chase effective.

To create a good chase scene, you need to sense that Harrison Ford is desperate to catch up with the basket, and that the people carrying it are desperate to get away. Simply cutting between shots of people running would not work well, even though many directors would resort to such simple tactics.

Spielberg sets the chase up by showing Ford trying to get an overview of the scene. Like us, Ford's character wants to know what's going on. Because there are other baskets in shot, and many people milling about, this framing lets us see his desperation, but also makes it clear that he's going to have problems. It's a brief moment, but the perfect setup for a difficult chase.

Before a pursuit begins, use an image that makes it look as though your hero's task is almost hopeless. The more visual barriers you put in front of your hero, the more tense you will make the audience feel.

Whether your hero is chasing another person, a car, or a basket, we need to get a clear shot of the prey escaping. This is achieved by showing the basket center-screen, and then panning with it as it moves away. The crowd in front of the basket again makes it look like there's a barrier in the way.

Whatever your hero is chasing, keep it framed centrally as it moves away so the audience has no doubt about what the hero is trying to catch.

Ford appears on the bottom left of the frame, pushing through a crowd that is all heading to the left of frame. This is an obvious barrier that slows him down and makes us eager for him to get on with the chase. Importantly, as he makes it through the crowd after much pushing and shoving, all the people turn away from the camera. This prevents us from watching their faces, because faces are always eye-catching. It also directs us to the empty space beyond to show Ford is now on his way.

If the hero begins the chase straight away, the audience will sense that it's all going to be over quickly, so put a barrier in the way.

We cut back to the basket, and again it is centrally framed. Spielberg is a master of directing attention, and this shot ensures that we see that the basket is clearly being rushed. To make the shot more dynamic, the camera is kept low so that it has to tilt up as the escapees approach.

Shooting from low down makes any approaching object or person appear to rush toward the camera, and helps add a sense of speed to the chase.

Stillness can be the key to conveying speed. When this shot opens, the camera does not move, so Ford's rapid burst into the alleyway contrasts with the stillness of the camera. He is halfway down the alley when the camera begins to pan with him, as though his movement is dragging it to the right.

To create a sense of motion, keep the camera still, but then as the hero approaches, pan to keep up.

The camera is low to the floor, which means that as Ford passes, it must tilt up to keep him in the frame. This exaggerates his speed and the pan itself. He glances to his left down an alleyway. His glance directs our attention to the existence of the alleyway.

Keep your camera low to exaggerate fast camera moves, and let your actor's performance direct the audience's attention.

Throughout this shot Ford's been frame left, but now the pan slows slightly and that causes him to move through the frame until he is frame right. It's as though we want to look down the alleyway, just as he does, but he's now sliding over to the right. This shot manages to build an enormous sense of speed, and then immediately makes us feel like the hero is going in the wrong direction.

To make the chase feel like it's going wrong, let your actor move across the frame at the precise moment that we see where the hero is really meant to be headed.

The shot continues by having the camera pan right over to show the alleyway that Ford was going to run down as he drags himself to a stop by grabbing onto a wall. Then the camera hesitates here, and we get a clear view of the alley, but Ford is a blur as he struggles to head across to the left of frame. The stillness of the camera, combined with his struggle, emphasizes his fight against the momentum he'd created by running at speed.

In the next frame he is back on the left of frame, and the background blurs as the camera follows him, showing that he is back on the move.

To underline a change in direction, let the camera come to a stop as the actor struggles to slow down, and then pan back to catch up with the actor.

This technique is repeated with a slight variation. As the camera pans to the left, it keeps moving with Ford until he bangs into the wall. A lesser director might have shown Ford heading straight down the alley, but giving him so much momentum that he slams into a wall gives a much better sense of him struggling to make his way through these streets. It lets the audience feel the impact and struggle to keep up speed. No matter how fast he goes, the going is difficult. The camera can then remain still as he runs into the distance.

Give your actor excessive momentum and let the camera follow as fast as possible, but then freeze when the actor bumps into another object or wall to make the chase look difficult.

This shot is an example of how efficiently Spielberg can make three story points in a matter of seconds with nothing more than a single pan to the right.

In the opening frame we see the basket, again centrally framed. This makes us focus on the basket, and it feels like another shot of the continuing chase. Ford is catching up in the background, but we only see him clearly when the basket escapes out to the right of frame. The audience subconsciously expects a cut to Ford in another part of town, but then he is revealed in the background, connecting him to the action and showing that the chase is going well.

Reveal your hero catching up in the background by having the escapees run out of the frame.

No sooner has Spielberg raised our expectations than he breaks them. The camera remains motionless until Ford begins to change direction. This slight delay, as we wait for him to catch up, helps build the expectation that we'll soon look to the right and see his quarry.

Wait for your hero to change direction before panning to create anticipation of what's around the corner.

The camera whip-pans to the right to reveal that the alley is empty, and the camera halts as Ford freezes. The entire setup is no more complex than placing a camera on a tripod and panning to the right, but it manages to lift our expectations and then break them.

When the hero comes to a halt, the camera also comes to a halt, to show that the hero is stuck.

We cut to a close-up of the back of Ford's head just as he whips around. The camera is lower than head height so that we're focused on his face rather than his surroundings.

When you need to see the actor's face, lower the camera a little so that tilting up hides the surroundings.

Although Ford is framed centrally, he is looking to frame right. This means that in the following shot, the subject should be placed to frame left. The next shot shows the end of the alleyway, with the basket passing by, and it is in the left of frame. The basket has been seen so many times now that showing it flick past a gap in the distance is a good way of making it seem comically out of reach.

Having the camera remain still and the quarry move past haphazardly can give you a moment of light relief while underlining that the chase is still on.

Ford runs out of his close-up, and we cut to a wide shot that we expect to progress as the others have done (with a whip-pan), but the camera remains almost stationary as Ford runs to the center of the frame before slowing down dramatically. It's obvious that he's seen something unexpected.

Have the actor rush forward and slow down in the center of frame, looking almost directly at the camera, to show a moment of surprise.

Unexpectedly, Ford doesn't come to a halt straight away, but rushes up so close to the camera that we can only see his eyes. This is a difficult trick to pull off. The actor needs to hit an exact mark on the ground, and the focus needs to be accurate. Even in this classic film they don't get it quite right, and it takes a moment for the shot to be in focus, but the effect is stunning. We have gone from a wide chase scene to a close-up of the hero's searching eyes without a single cut.

When you want to see an actor's reaction, without dialogue, place the camera close to the actor's eyes. If you can do it without cutting, the effect is even more powerful.

As his eyes search, the audience is desperate for a cut to the reverse angle to see what he's looking at, but Spielberg holds the tension by having the camera dolly back away from Ford. He looks to frame left, which is empty, and it appears as though the chase is about to continue.

When the audience thinks you're about to show what the actor is looking at, you can stretch out the tension by dollying back from your actor.

As Ford runs into the empty space on frame left, we pan with him, but not as fast as he moves. This moves him from frame right to frame left, which creates a sudden burst of motion.

To create the impression of great speed, pan so that you don't quite keep up, and have the actor cross the frame completely.

The pan continues to the left, and Ford moves into a crowd filled with people carrying many baskets identical to the one he's been chasing. You probably can't use this exact visual gag, but you can show your hero moving into an unexpected space or location, or facing a host of unexpected foes. By panning as the hero runs into the problem, and away from the camera, you make the chase seem futile, and the hero's dilemma appears to be insurmountable.

CHAPTER 2

GUIDING THE EYE:
E.T. the Extra-Terrestrial

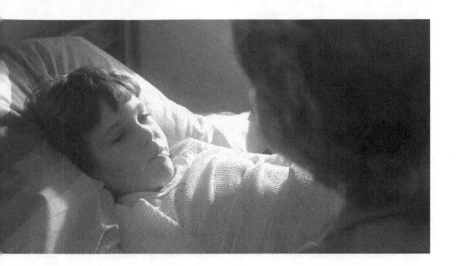

IF SPIELBERG HAS A SIGNATURE MOVE, it's using objects and people to guide the camera around a space. This is far more than a gimmick or a stylistic trick. It is a way of ensuring that the audience is looking in the right place, and it creates a sense of flow rather than a series of endless cuts. This flow can make for better storytelling.

Another benefit of this technique is that you can make small and potentially boring spaces more visually fascinating. In this scene, the audience should feel tense. We know Henry Thomas wants to stay home with the alien in his cupboard, and is faking sickness. A conventional shoot, with lots of cuts, could have left this scene flat, but Spielberg pushes and pulls our gaze around the scene to bring it to life.

The opening shot is a traditional over-the-shoulder shot, but the most important story point — that Thomas is unwell — is made clear by the image of the thermometer.

Open your scene with a visual clue as to what's going to follow.

Before cutting to a wider shot that shows us the room, Dee Wallace takes the thermometer out, and although our focus stays on Thomas, we can see the thermometer clearly. With the scene now set, we cut back to a wider shot of the room. The wide shot lets us see exactly where this scene is taking place, but the characters are also framed by the arms of the lamp in the foreground. Given that the lamp is about to play an important part in guiding our eye, it's important to get it into the frame now rather than have it intrude unexpectedly.

When you're using an object to guide the eye through a scene, make sure that the object is visible when you cut to the shot.

Wallace turns away from the camera and heads out of the room. The lens is so wide that the room seems quite large, and her movement away from the camera is exaggerated, making her appear to leave the room rapidly. The lamp, on the left of screen, is out of focus but impossible to miss.

Rather than cutting to a different shot of somebody leaving the room, follow the characters out with a pan, and let that pan end on the object you're using to guide the eye.

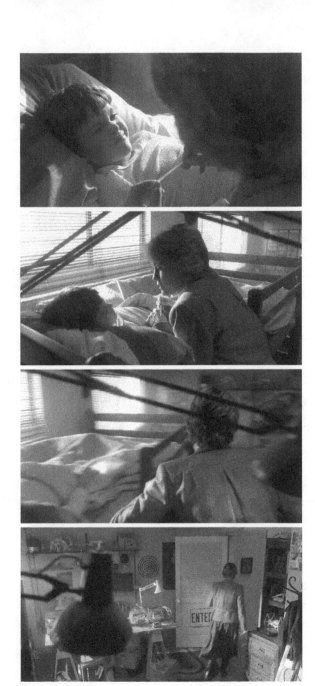

Before Wallace has fully disappeared from frame, the lamp begins to swing out of frame. For a moment the camera doesn't move, then pans rapidly to catch up with it. We have just panned to the right, following her out, and now this motion drags the camera back to the left. We see Thomas is pulling the lamp over his bed. Panning right and panning back to the left, without something to guide our eye, would feel very abrupt and distracting. The movement of the lamp gives a reason to pan back so sharply, and causes no distraction.

With one setup and a simple pan in two directions, you can show an entire room and return to your original setup — but you need something or someone to move through the scene to guide the eye.

In the next frame we see Thomas touch his thermometer to the lamp to heat it up, which explains why the lamp was being pulled over in the first place. These moves are always more effective when they are following story points. Some directors attempt to copy Spielberg, and have objects moving through scenes to guide the eye, but the objects have nothing to do with the story. To make these moves work, everything that guides the eye should contribute to the story being told in the scene.

We cut back to the original framing to see Thomas cover his face for a moment, and then begin to push the lamp away. Although the entire scene could have been shot wide, it's good to see the actor's face and expression, so make sure you shoot the whole scene from this angle.

Many things may move in your scene, but only some are vital to the story. Build your camera moves around the objects that contribute to the story.

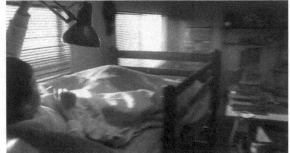

Holding the close-up on Thomas for a moment lets us see him push the lamp out of the frame so that when we cut back to the wide shot, the lamp is already in motion, and we pan right again. Re-creating the previous setup that follows the lamp, just as Wallace returns, is quite comical.

When you've used an object to motivate the camera move once, you can repeat the exact move later in the scene for comedic effect.

More importantly, however, this action of swinging right and left and back again has set up a rhythm, and this builds expectation. We now expect Wallace to head back to the bed, and for the camera to pan with her. Instead, she moves to the right of frame and heads to the cupboard, the one place that Thomas doesn't want her to go. By setting up a rhythm and then breaking it, Spielberg makes this moment of disaster much more unexpected. We're so busy following the backward and forward motion as he schemes to appear unwell that we forget about the cupboard in which the alien is hiding. The camera pans right with Wallace, breaking the rhythm so that we are pulled out of the brief feeling of comedy. This creates instant fear.

When you create a visual rhythm with your camera moves, you can break that rhythm to create a sudden moment of shock or suspense.

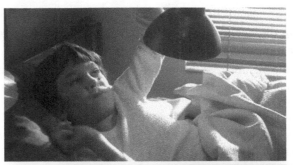

Spielberg now switches to an entirely different technique for guiding the eye, using shadow and light, keeping the camera almost completely still. Despite the lack of motion in the camera, this setup ensures we are looking where the director wants us to look, and imagining what he wants us to imagine.

The initial framing shows that we are in the cupboard, behind the hanging clothes. We know this is where E.T. is hiding, so we're afraid there will be a discovery. The last thing we want is for Wallace to peek through those clothes, so Spielberg takes this to an extreme and has her fling them to either side of the screen so that she dominates the frame. Keeping her in silhouette makes this moment more frightening than if we could see her face.

When you keep the camera still, use sudden movement to reveal new visuals. One of the best ways is to have an object or person swept out of the frame to reveal a character.

As she moves into the room, we expect that we'll cut to a shot from the reverse angle to see what she's seeing in the cupboard. Instead, she walks past the camera, leaving the bright glare of the window as the only thing we can see. Thomas then sits up, obscuring that glare, and we see him looking anxiously into the cupboard. He is so small in the frame that he appears vulnerable. Without moving the camera or cutting, Spielberg creates strong tension and makes the audience eager to see what's going on in the cupboard.

When the audience expects a cut, have a character in the distant background become more visible so that we watch him or her and share the character's anguish.

CHAPTER 3

REVEALING IDEAS:
Jurassic Park

T HE SCENES THAT SOUND SIMPLE ON paper are often the most difficult to shoot. In this scene, we've already seen an establishing shot of archaeologists digging up dinosaur bones, but Spielberg needs to introduce the main characters. We need to see that they are a couple in charge of this operation. We also need to understand that modern techniques are being used to send shock-waves into the ground, which are then analyzed by a computer.

Although this information is important to the story, it isn't exactly gripping, so Spielberg had to find a way to make it visually interesting, and most importantly, fast. This entire sequence of shots lasts no more than thirty seconds. It works by using a mix of reasonably long takes with no cuts, and sequences of rapid cuts. Combined, these convey all the information we need.

The scene opens with an establishing shot of the location, showing the dinosaur dig in the background, and a man coming toward camera.

Establishing shots should do more than show where the scene is about to take place. They set the mood and show all the important details that will be needed later in the sequence.

After an establishing shot like this we expect a cut to the character who's being addressed, but Spielberg keeps the scene more interesting by having Sam Neill stand up in the frame, close to the camera, and we pull focus to his face in the center of the screen. By having him break into the frame, with everything else vanishing behind him and going out of focus, he is immediately established as the main character.

This move only works because it's plausible for an archeologist to be scrambling around on the ground, so make sure you have a good reason for getting your actor to rise up like this. The effect works almost as well if an actor moves in from the side.

To give your main character a strong introduction, get the actor to move into an establishing shot.

Neill is now joined by Laura Dern, although we do not see her face immediately. She ties a scarf around his neck. This serves a story point of showing that Neill's character is perhaps a little self-involved and concerned only about his own problems, but also gives Dern a motivation to move into frame. If she merely walked up to him to talk, it would look strange, so she needs a reason to physically get close for her appearance to be plausible.

When introducing a second character into the same frame, give them a reason to get physically close. It can be something intimate, such as a kiss, or something practical, as shown in this example.

The sequence that follows the introduction of these characters contains a lot of fast cutting, so it's a good idea to shoot this scene without edits. The danger is that we will not see Dern's face, so Spielberg has her set off down the hill first. This means that we see Neill in profile, and as Dern looks back at him, we see her face. We sense the connection between the two of them, and have now been introduced to the two major characters.

When shooting without cuts, get one actor to move away from the camera first so that character has a reason to look back toward camera.

As they move down the hill, they embrace, meaning the shot ends almost as it began. Instead of the distant figure heading up the hill, we now see these two figures heading down as one. Having them move off close together (rather than walking with a gap between them) reflects the establishing shot, and helps remind us they're heading down to the area we saw in that shot.

This setup is an example of how Spielberg creates a complex sequence without any camera moves other than slight tilts. All the work is done through careful positioning of the actors.

Echo the opening of the scene as closely as possible to show that your characters are being pulled into the story.

To establish the area that our heroes are heading down to, Spielberg shows an extreme close-up of a machine. What appears to be a shotgun cartridge is lowered into a slot. This grabs our attention and tells us that some sort of loud bang is coming. Science experiments can look very boring onscreen, no matter how fast your cuts, so any sense of danger you can introduce helps.

When you're showing something new or unusual, an extreme close-up of something familiar within that scene helps draw the audience into the sequence.

Having started with a close-up, the director now needs to reveal that two men are standing on a strange machine that has some sort of platform pressed close to the ground. Rather than cutting to a wide shot, Spielberg jump cuts a little further back and then uses motion to guide our eye down. The actor on the left pushes a lever forward with his left hand, which guides our eye to his right hand. His right hand then drops, and the camera follows. As his right hand reaches for another lever, the camera's momentum continues until it reveals the strange machine on which they are standing.

This wouldn't work if the camera was too far back, so make sure you get close enough that following the motion causes the camera to point down at the ground. You can resist shooting everything wide, and always trying to show faces. The characters here are not paramount; focusing on the details of the machine is more important.

A quick series of movements within the scene gives the camera something to follow, enabling you to reveal the details of any device, machine, or object you want to show to the audience.

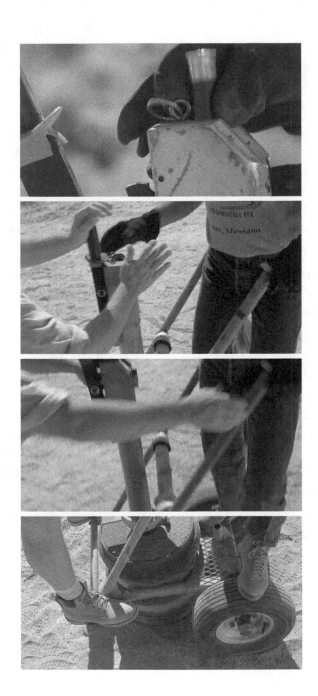

We cut back to the original shot to see a pin being pulled out of the machine. This could just as easily be a button, key, or switch, but it's important to film this moment where the machine is fired so the audience knows there hasn't been an accident.

Spielberg could have missed out on this sequence with the machine and simply had the characters walk up to a computer screen to see the readouts. The inclusion of the machine was probably not for realism, but to add a little burst of energy to a scene that could otherwise be dull. Neill's character is not fond of this modern approach to archaeology, so this sequence does make story sense and helps reveal his character.

If there's any danger that a sequence could be dull, add visual interest with some rapid cuts, but make sure the visuals are tied to the story or character.

The camera is now low and close to the machine so that when the machine fires, the burst of dirt almost fills the screen. This leaves us in no doubt as to what has happened. It is only now, after a series of rapid shots of the machine itself, that we cut to a wide shot. The traditional approach of showing a wide and then going in close would have made the machine more significant than it needed to be. By shooting close then going wide, we see that the machine being fired is a background activity that others are watching.

After rapid close-ups, a wide of the same moment introduces the audience to the new location.

Sam Neill now walks into the wide shot before the dust settles, and the camera tilts up to look at him. By having the camera low, we are able to tilt away from the small explosion, and this reinforces that it's his response to this situation that is important.

Put the camera low down so that you tilt up to show your actor, placing the focus upon the character rather than the background action.

When Neill turns away from the machine, the camera dollies back to reveal a man looking at computer screens, and we see more of the crowd gathering around. Neill moves off to the right of frame. His face is in view as we see him turning to face the screen. Dern enters the frame on the left, moves over to the right, and the camera comes to a rest. We can now see the man with the computers, the background crowd, and Neill and Dern looking on. With one dolly move, the director was able to show a wide of the machine, introduce our characters, and draw them into another, richer part of the location.

Rather than cutting to another angle, dolly back through the scene, revealing previously unseen details as you go, and have characters crowd into the frame.

CHAPTER 4

VISUAL REVEALS:
Empire of the Sun

I N THIS SEQUENCE FROM *Empire of the Sun*, Christian Bale discovers a crashed plane. The character has already seen planes flying overhead, but this is the moment when he first makes physical contact with a war machine. In a film that is partly about the potential loss of innocence, this contact needs to have as much visual impact on the audience as it does on the character. We need to feel the sense of wonder and awe that a boy would, but as an audience we should also feel a little more dread and anguish than he because we know that danger is being foreshadowed.

For this to work, Spielberg needs to take Bale on a journey from pure innocence to a place where he confronts the world of war. The scene opens with a tiny airplane flying overhead, which offers an important contrast to the big visuals of a plane that will follow.

When you're about to reveal a big image, foreshadow it with similar imagery at the start of the scene. This can be done with photographs, drawings, models, or other images that subtly hint at what is to come.

When your character makes a discovery that has the potential to change their world, you should establish their current world-view first. The script sets this scene at a party and has Bale play with a toy plane, and Spielberg ensures that these visuals are skillfully emphasized. The shot begins with the camera dollying to the left, with Bale hidden by the party festivities, and then the camera comes to a rest as he emerges and stands, looking up at the off-screen plane. Ahead of him there is open space, suggesting he could move off in that direction. An adult joins him, but he continues to gaze at the sky. He is still in the world of a child — at a party, holding a toy, overlooked by an adult, but with the world before him ready to be explored.

A single camera move can shift your character from their ordinary world to the threshold of a new reality. This works best if you leave relatively empty space in front of your actor.

When Bale runs to the left, the camera pans to follow him, and we catch a few last glimpses of the surrounding party as he rushes through. Moments later we see the countryside ahead of him, and only a few party lanterns hanging on the right of frame. This is a strong contrast to the party scene, and it's as though he's deliberately fleeing from his ordinary world. He remains blissfully unaware of this, and is still playing with his toy plane. This creates a slight sense of foreboding for the audience. He's running away from normality, but still has the innocence of a child.

To create a sense of mild dread, set up scenes so that a pan to follow the character reveals a scene that has a contrasting dramatic tone.

Using an extremely long lens, Spielberg films Bale running toward camera with his plane. He runs to the left of frame, but a slight pan keeps him at the same position in the frame. The long lens makes it look like he's running in one place rather than moving forward. This, combined with the continual reframing, gives a momentary sensation that Bale is trapped. The camera is so low that we can't even see his feet, as though he is stuck to the ground, unable to fly. He clearly dreams of flying, but he's making no progress. This brief sensation of being grounded enables the director to create contrast in the next shot.

To make your character seem momentarily suspended or unable to make progress, use a long lens and pan to keep the actor at the same place in the frame.

We cut to a shot of Bale releasing the plane. The focus is now on the plane rather than him, so when the shot begins, it almost fills the frame. The camera tilts up to follow the plane as Bale moves completely out of shot. We cut back to the original running shot, but Bale now jumps joyfully into the air, free of his previous constraints. The long-held plane has been released, and so has the boy.

To show your character making a mental or emotional breakthrough, create a shot that shows a physical change that echoes that breakthrough.

We see a brief shot of the adults chatting at the party before cutting to a shot of the toy plane flying in from the left of frame. We pan with the plane until Bale appears, and the camera stops when he is framed centrally. The plane flies out of view.

Spielberg's signature technique of following an object to reveal a person works especially well here, because we can tell from Bale's expression that he has already seen something off-screen. We don't see his moment of discovery, but we see that he's turned his back on the toy that meant so much to him seconds before. This indicates that he's looking at something of great significance.

To show the audience that a major discovery has been made, have the character literally turn away from a previous obsession. Whatever the character sees should remain unseen by the audience.

The camera dollies back as Bale walks forward, and as soon as the wingtip comes into view, we guess what he's looking at. It feels as though we'll keep moving back for a full reveal, but Spielberg tantalizes us a little longer by having Bale stop, and the camera comes to a rest with him.

Hold back the reveal as long as you can by having the character pause to look at the partially seen object.

The next cut is a shock, because although the scene has included a lot of movement, the reveal of the plane was gradual and incomplete. Cutting to a full wide shot, with Bale appearing tiny in the frame, gives us a visual jolt and a moment of wonder.

When you're revealing something gradually, cut to a wider shot to create impact.

As Bale climbs onto the wing, the camera dollies down the plane's left-hand side, and pans left to keep Bale roughly in the same part of the frame. At the last moment, he speeds up and moves toward the center of frame. This lets us share his feeling of cautious approach, and then his leap to get closer.

Dolly at a ninety-degree angle to your subject, and pan to keep the actor framed to one side. When you get close to the object, the actor can rush faster than you are panning to show a breakthrough.

The later part of this scene shows Bale climbing into the plane and pretending to fly, so Spielberg frames him through the plane's canopy to visually suggest that he is already in the plane.

You can also emphasize a character's intention to enter an object or location by framing the actor through the object or location.

CHAPTER 5

DYNAMIC DIALOGUE:

Jaws

THERE IS A LOT OF TALKING IN *Jaws*, and not a lot of shark. For the shark moments to work well, we need to know and care about the characters' personal dramas. Spielberg keeps the shark out of sight and lets the characters talk. The director doesn't stop the action to let the characters talk, but has them struggle through their dialogue while surrounded by distractions and problems.

Spielberg needs to show Roy Scheider isolated and yet surrounded by chaos. The film is largely about Scheider trying to connect with the residents of the town, so he puts Scheider in a room away from the people. He's also talking on the phone to show that he's cut off from direct contact with people. Spielberg also frames things so that the scene is shot with a minimal number of cuts, using careful blocking to keep things moving.

When your character is feeling isolated or in danger, shoot from behind and show the actor looking out on the chaos beyond.

Once Scheider has looked out of the window, we need to see the rest of the room where the scene will take place, so Scheider turns around sharply while continuing his phone conversation. His movement enables the camera to pan quickly to the left without it feeling like a sudden camera move. We get to see Scheider's face briefly before the camera comes to a stop.

Have your character turn around so their face is close to the camera, and use their motion to reveal a new part of the location.

When the camera stops, Scheider looks directly toward the window, guiding the audience to peer out of the window at Jeffrey Kramer standing outside. This connects the internal space to the outside. Scheider looks to the left of frame, and then leans over to grab a handful of unseen objects before peering back out of the window. This has the effect of putting Scheider in the center of frame, visually close to Kramer. Although this moment is brief, it heightens the sense of frustration he's feeling. Even when he's right next to somebody in the frame, he can't make contact.

When characters are separated by a physical barrier, such as a window, place them close together in the frame to underline that they remain out of contact.

Kramer's casual detachment from the scene is a contrast to every-thing else that's happening in this part of the film, so Scheider throws the objects he's picked up directly at the window. He moves back to the right of frame, so we get a clear view of Kramer turning to face the camera and waving. Scheider waves him inside while still facing away from the camera because we are focused on Kramer.

When you draw attention to a character in the background, make sure your foreground character turns away from the camera.

As Kramer heads to the door and out of shot, Scheider turns so that we see his face in profile. This carefully timed move lets us see his anguish as he continues the phone conversation. He then moves even further back, providing a clear view of Kramer entering through the door in the exact center of the frame.

When one character is about to come through a door, move the other character to the side of the frame before the door opens.

Spielberg needs to configure the actors so that they are in the classic face-to-face position without the shot appearing artificial. To solve this, the director has Scheider reach over to pull the cigarette from Kramer's mouth. Giving the actor a reason to move is better than having them walk up to predetermined marks simply because that's where you want them to be.

If you need to move your actors into position, give the character a reason to move so that the repositioning appears to be natural.

Because there's a lot of space between the characters, the reverse angle on Scheider is quite unusual, but Spielberg maintains interest by having Kramer look to his right while discussing what's going on outside, letting us see both faces at once.

If you use a single over-the-shoulder shot, rather than cutting between two, find a way to get the foreground character's face into the frame.

The actors are now positioned so that the door behind them is centrally framed, but there is no indication it's going to be opened, which makes the appearance of Richard Dreyfuss more interesting. The other actors turn away from the camera completely so that we see his face most clearly at this moment. Until this moment, other characters have largely ignored Dreyfuss, and letting him be the only face in frame makes it clear that he has an important part to play.

An additional character's appearance in a scene can be emphasized by having the other actors turn away from the camera.

Long dialogue scenes will often be split into thematic sections, functioning as two mini scenes. As Kramer leaves, all the characters turn their backs to the camera to indicate that this part of the scene is over. Dreyfuss then turns around, facing the camera and framed centrally once more, but Scheider turns away from him and again heads off to the right. If they had simply started talking, the flow of this scene would have stopped, so it's important to keep up the visual momentum by having Scheider turn away.

When your scene is flowing, keep one of your actors on the move to ensure the momentum of the dialogue doesn't grind to a halt.

As Scheider moves we pan with him, and Dreyfuss moves in close as though following him. This serves the story in several ways. It shows that Scheider is still struggling with the chaos and the phone call; it shows Dreyfuss struggling to be heard; and it also puts both in the correct position for another face-to-face conversation. This time, the actors are closer to camera, but when Scheider turns back around we can see them make eye contact and talk.

When an additional conversation takes place in the same room, have the actors move to a new position to avoid shooting the second conversation with the same framing as the first.

At this point Spielberg could easily cut to over-the-shoulder shots, but some masterful blocking gets the scene to work without any cuts. As the characters shake hands, Scheider moves around so that we can see his face, and Dreyfuss is now in profile. There is no reason for him to move around, but by having the movement occur during a handshake, it appears natural.

Let us see both characters' faces, but use motions such as handshakes or the exchange of objects to disguise these movements.

Scheider now moves over to the right of frame to shuffle some objects around off-screen. Again, we never see what he's doing with his hands, and we don't need to know, but this gives room for Dreyfuss to move around and face the camera. When Scheider turns back to him, they are once again face-to-face. Finally, as Scheider leaves, they settle briefly in the profile position. In a long dialogue scene, we want to see both actors' faces, and this careful blocking ensures that we do see them both without their movements seeming forced.

You can sustain a long dialogue scene if you keep your actors moving, and position them so that we see both faces without having to cut to different angles.

CHAPTER 6

WAVES OF
SUSPENSE:
Catch Me If You Can

S PIELBERG USES WAVES OF tension and relief to build the overall suspense in this scene. By letting the tension build, relaxing it, and building it back up again, the audience feels a great sense of anticipation. It's never clear what's going to come next.

At this point in the film, as the detectives walk with determination through the hotel grounds, it looks as though Tom Hanks is about to catch Leonardo DiCaprio, but it's far too early in the film for that to happen. The audience knows it's too soon for the climax, which is why so much care has to be put into this scene. Without excruciating tension, the audience might sit back and assume that everything's going to be alright because there's at least another hour to go before the credits roll.

If the audience can guess how a scene will probably end, raise and lower the tension throughout to create a sense of fascinating uncertainty.

Hanks appears at the bottom of the staircase, alone, small in the frame and apparently nervous, in complete contrast to the previous shot. As he climbs the stairs, the camera tilts up, but then slows so that we can see him fumbling with his gun. Already Spielberg has begun to alternate between certainty and uncertainty. Hanks looked confident a moment ago, but now appears anxious about his mission.

Once you've established a confident, fast-moving character, cut to a shot of the same character moving in a stealthy, vulnerable way to unsettle the audience.

In classic Spielberg style, we follow the gun as Hanks pushes it ahead, but the camera stops when we see the worker in the background. Hanks holds up his FBI documents, obscuring her face. By presenting Hanks with a barrier, we wonder if his pursuit will be as easy as it first seemed.

Put small obstructions in the way of your characters so the audience will begin to fear that unexpected events are ahead.

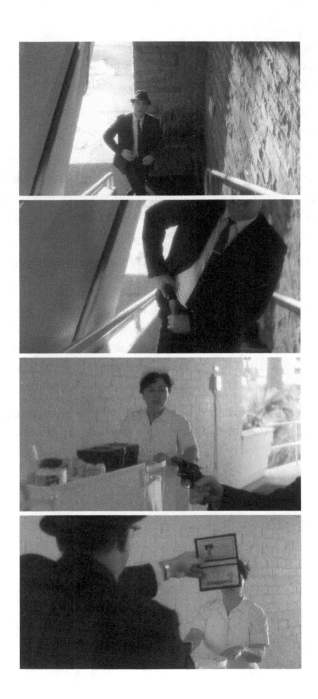

The camera pans left as Hanks heads into the corridor, but does not move with him. By leaving the camera in place, and having him move away, we sense him moving into dangerous territory.

After a moment of surprise, keep the camera still and let your character be swallowed by the location.

We cut to a reverse, with a silhouetted Hanks heading toward the camera, and the camera now dollies backward. Moving backward is highly unsettling for an audience. We cut back to a shot from behind Hanks, and this camera is dollying forward. Once movement has been introduced, it's easier to cut between moving shots.

To make the audience feel uneasy, dolly backward during at least one shot.

The next shot shows only the gun, with Hanks moving forward as the camera continues to dolly backward. He begins to turn toward the open space on the left of frame. It is a Hollywood convention that when a star is in a scene we see their face, so hiding Hanks' face creates the subtle sensation that something is amiss.

To unnerve the audience, hide the actor's face by shooting from behind, at a low level, or using low lighting and silhouettes.

The camera keeps moving back, and Hanks comes fully into view as he approaches the door. We pause just long enough to see that the door is unlocked and partially open. This is not a barrier so much as an invitation, and we expect Hanks to storm into the room.

Doors are usually barriers in films, but seeing one left half-open is an uneasy invitation.

From inside the room we see Hanks burst into frame, and the handheld camera rushes toward him. This brief but dramatic shot gives us the momentary sensation that he's being attacked. The camera swings around to follow Hanks, and we see him looking around an empty room. At the moment when we were certain there would be action, Spielberg surprises us with an apparent anticlimax.

Once you've created tension, relieve it for a moment with some form of anticlimax. This enables the tension to rise again soon after.

The camera whips around and moves down to look at the traces of forgery left behind by DiCaprio. This tells us that he was here, but now he appears to have gone. We never get a full shot of the room, and this keeps the audience disoriented.

Shoot small details rather than showing a wide shot of the whole room to confuse the viewer before establishing the new location.

A cut to floor level shows traces of a hastily cleared room, including potato chips on the floor. When Hanks stands on a chip, we cut to a camera that's pointing down at his feet. In a flash, the camera tilts up to show Hanks, who is looking down to see what he stepped on. These rapid shots serve to increase confusion and disorientation. A noise in the bathroom makes him turn around 180 degrees, and we cut to a close-up. The gun is in the center of the frame, completely out of focus, and all our attention is on Hanks' expression.

A series of rapid cuts and camera moves works best if it is followed by a steady close-up that lets us see the character's fear.

Having established that Hanks is afraid, we cut to a handheld shot from behind him so that we can see the bathroom door. A shot like this makes the audience expect some sort of action, either through the door or from an unexpected angle, so it shouldn't be held for too long.

When you've shown the character's fear, let us see what he's looking at. Shoot from behind the actor to create a brief feeling of vulnerability.

The next shot is also handheld, and shows Hanks moving toward the bathroom door while giving orders. The last thing we expect is for DiCaprio to open the door calmly, but he does, and then pokes his head around the corner. He faces Hanks and raises his finger, making us flinch as we assume he will get shot.

The remainder of this long scene plays out in a similar fashion, with expectations built up and broken down repeatedly, so that we remain anxious until the final cut.

When the story allows it, show one character remaining completely calm while another is on the verge of panic. The contrast makes it impossible to guess how the scene will end, and that creates ongoing suspense.

CHAPTER 7

DEPTH STAGING:
Schindler's List

THE CAMERA MOVES IN this scene could be achieved on any low-budget shoot. With nothing more than a dolly and pan, Spielberg manages to create a devastatingly powerful scene. It is a masterpiece of efficient, dramatic storytelling.

By shooting without cuts, we remain aware of the concentration camp in the background, we watch a conflict take place, and we even see an actor in extreme close-up. This enables us to sense the physical depth of the location while feeling the tension build through the actors' performances.

The opening frame appears to be an establishing shot, but we notice Elina Löwensohn in the center of the frame, shouting at the construction workers. Norbert Weisser heads toward camera, also shouting, and the momentum of the scene builds.

Start your scene with a wide shot, but rather than cutting away, move the actors toward camera so you can stage the scene in front of the background you've established.

As Weisser continues his move toward camera, we dolly backward and see Ralph Fiennes being catered to by another guard. By passing close to the actors, this gives us a chance to see Fiennes in medium close-up, being pampered with a warm drink, while the workers toil in the background. Spielberg is always careful to give his actors something physical to do at these moments so that it never feels like they are merely standing there waiting for the scene to begin.

When you dolly away from the establishing shot, let the other actors come into view, but stage it so they're involved with their own business. This makes it more interesting when they are drawn into the scene.

The camera comes to a rest as Weisser takes his place in the frame. A background actor runs across from frame right to left, and this draws our eye to the bellowing Löwensohn, who heads toward camera. A guard moves into the right of the shot to give it balance. Without him standing there, the frame would feel too empty on the right. This backward dolly has also revealed more workers in the midground on the right. With one short dolly move, the scene is transformed from an overview of a construction site to a crowd of soldiers watching the site foreman approach.

Don't be afraid to stage your actors some distance from the camera. Keep the dolly moving back so there is room for the actors to interact, and space to see the depth of the background action.

Although Löwensohn is small in the frame, all the focus is now on her pleas because her face is the most clearly visible, and all eyes are on her. The camera has been put at a height that makes it obvious how much the guards tower over her.

When you want the audience to focus on a particular character, have all the other characters look at the actor.

She looks back at the construction site and it feels like an extremely well-populated area. If you count the number of extras in this scene, there are very few. By placing small crowds from the midground to the distance, Spielberg uses a minimal number of background actors to create the sense of a large workforce.

Even low-budget scenes can be made to look crowded by layering your background actors in groups from the midground to the distance.

Löwensohn moves around so that we see her in profile. This movement is motivated by her eagerness to introduce herself to Fiennes, but enables him to turn so that we can see his face in profile. The focus is no longer on her, but on the conflict building between the two of them.

Move your actors so that all faces are visible during the scene, but make these moves at moments of change or revelation in the dialogue to ensure the movement is plausible.

Fiennes walks away to check on her claims about the construction site, and although he shrinks in the frame, we see him moving into her territory, invading the space she previously occupied, which underlines his power in this situation.

Moving a villain into the distance can be an effective way of showing the power they hold over the entire location.

Fiennes calls the other officer to join him; this leaves Löwensohn vulnerable. She is no longer somebody being spoken to, but somebody being discussed. Fiennes casually orders her execution, an action that is far more chilling when done from a distance.

During a conflict we expect the two parties to remain in conflict, but you can create intense drama by having the villain give casual orders from a distance.

As Weisser moves toward Löwensohn and takes her by the arm, the camera pushes toward them, stopping only when Fiennes calls for her to be shot in front of the other workers. This sudden shift from a wide shot to a close-up is horrific, and echoes the way her character's world has just shrunk. She is no longer looking at the huge construction site (which is now blurred in the background), but is brought face-to-face with her fate.

At a moment of intense drama, you can push the camera right up to an actor and use the close-up to underline the character's shock.

She turns to face Fiennes and the focus shifts to him so that we can see him unmoved by what he has suggested. She is dragged off to the left, with Fiennes following. The camera pushes forward again, panning to the left. This enables us to follow the characters, but also brings the soldier on the left — nervously drinking from his cup, apparently uneasy with this turn of events — into the foreground. This push and pan also changes our view of the location completely, almost as though we have cut to another angle.

Rather than simply following the action, use the move to reveal new details in the foreground, and to give a new perspective on the location.

As Weisser drags Löwensohn over the track to the right of frame, Fiennes crosses to the left of frame. By having him cross to the left as they move to the right, we get a strong sense of motion. Nobody is moving fast, but the crisscrossing makes the pace of the scene feel rapid.

Stage your scenes so that there is plenty of movement across the frame, as well as moving actors toward and away from the camera. This makes the scene feel like it has been shot from many angles, even though it is a single take.

CHAPTER 8

SYMBOLIC HEIGHTS:

Amistad

ONE OF THE BEST WAYS to add visual interest to your scene is to place your camera, or your actor, at an unusual height. Spielberg employs this technique frequently, and when used well it does more than make the framings more interesting. Changes of height can show character and story development on a symbolic level.

This scene is written well and acted beautifully, but if it had been shot with the characters all on one level, talking to each other with the camera at head height, it would have lost most of its grandeur.

The opening frame shows the status quo we have come to expect for Djimon Hounsou at this point in the film. The camera looks down on him to reflect the oppressive circumstances of his imprisonment.

Use camera height and actor positioning to add visual interest, but always consider the story points before making these choices.

The reverse angle is an over-the-shoulder shot, slightly lower than Hounsou's head height. This means we look up at the other actors as the table is brought in. In the second frame, Matthew McConaughey approaches the table, and although he is distant, he remains standing, and this shows him to be the one in control of this meeting. He is there to help, but we do not see him as a noble savior because he is being filmed from Hounsou's point of view. He feels more like an intruder, and we are wary of what he has to offer.

Shoot from below the head height of your viewpoint character to make the other characters dominate the frame even when they are distant.

Chiwetel Ejiofor moves from behind the table and approaches the camera so that he now dominates proceedings as he translates the conversation. The next shot is not from head height, looking down at Hounsou, but from hip height, so that we can see Ejiofor's motioning hands. Placing the camera at head height would be too extreme, making it feel like Ejiofor was an enemy rather than a translator, so this level is a good compromise. We are still above Hounsou, to sense his oppression, but it is kept subtle. Also, the image of gesturing hands becomes important later in the scene.

Aim to be slightly above the character so the audience can connect to their feelings rather than merely look down on them.

McConaughey brings the chair from behind the table, showing that he is attempting to bypass the barrier of convention that separates the characters. When he sits, Ejiofor crouches, and Morgan Freeman moves to fill the space on the left of frame. This composition, with the three heads forming a diagonal line toward Hounsou, emphasizes their focus on him. Such a composition could only be achieved by using a combination of low camera heights, with actors at various heights and distances. Although a beautiful composition, it works because it enhances the intensity of their concentration on Hounsou.

Strange framing makes use of diagonal lines to enhance a scene, and it is easier to create these lines when you combine unusual camera and actor heights.

The reverse on Hounsou is shot from hip height, but because McConaughey is seated, we now see the two appearing to be almost on the same level. It is as though communication is being established. When McConaughey sits back in his chair, the height change is not dramatic but he shrinks in the frame, and this makes him look less imposing than when he leaned forward.

Keep your camera in the same place and block the actors' movements to show the change in the relationships between the characters.

When the conversation takes a turn that unnerves Hounsou, he stands and crosses the frame. His silhouette briefly covers the two actors on the left of frame, and he then passes McConaughey. At this moment, McConaughey turns, and we cut to a close-up of him from the opposite direction to see him turn. The close-up is shot from his head height to show that we are now seeing the scene from his point of view.

Get a seated character to stand, and move the camera to the head height of the other character. This shifts our viewpoint to the second character.

The next shot gives us McConaughey's view of Hounsou standing by the prison doors, and although Hounsou is facing away from the camera, we are looking up at him. As he tells the story, he begins to dominate the scene. The shot of Freeman further emphasizes that we are no longer looking down, but we have switched point of view to look up from McConaughey's level. Whether the audience is conscious of this or not, they will feel the dynamic of the scene change.

When you have changed the dynamic of a scene, ensure that you shoot everybody from this camera height to give a cohesive viewpoint.

Hounsou turns to face the camera, and walks forward. To keep him in frame the camera has to tilt up, further emphasizing his dominance of the scene. He comes so close that the camera tilts up so that we can only see the roof, and the prison bars are no longer visible. Although he is talking about his lack of real power, in this moment he is the one controlling the action.

Place your camera so that it doesn't feel too low, but then tilt up when an actor approaches to show how that character is the focus of the scene.

From this position Hounsou takes a step forward and leans down, facing the left of frame. This height change brings Freeman into the background, which prevents Hounsou from feeling too isolated. It is important for us to feel him connecting to the others. His head is still higher in the frame than Freeman's, showing that even when he leans down, we are all looking up at him.

The smallest height change can completely alter the scene, so experiment with actor blocking, but ensure the dominant character remains highest in the frame.

The final shot of McConaughey shows him centrally framed, almost stooping as he listens, with Hounsou filling the right of the frame. On the left, Ejiofor's hands gesture above McConaughey. When the conversation began, his hands were above Hounsou, so this shows the change in dynamic that has occurred during the scene.

Small visual clues, planted earlier in the scene, can help to reflect the dialogue. Used well, these can transform the scene into something extraordinary.

CHAPTER 9

RAPID STORYTELLING:
Amistad

A HALLMARK OF SPIELBERG'S TECHNIQUE is his ability to convey several vital story points in a matter of seconds. In the more impressive scenes, this is done without a word of dialogue.

The previous scene to this one in *Amistad* ended with the revelation of bad news, and the opening frame of this scene shows Matthew McConaughey reacting, swiping papers from his desk, toward camera.

The following sequence shows the gravity of the situation, a journey to seek aid and a potential solution, all in under twenty-five seconds.

When you want to tell story rapidly, start the scene with a bang. Have something smash, break, or fly toward camera to indicate that rapid change is underway.

Rather than showing McConaughey hearing the news, reacting, discussing, and planning, we simply see him react. As the papers fly off the end of the desk, we cut to a wider shot. Morgan Freeman is seated because the camera is tilted down toward McConaughey, who is lower than usual because he is close to the desk.

Even in extremely short scenes, allow for some camera movement. Start with your actors low down and angle the camera onto them.

As the papers fly off the desk, Freeman stands, with McConaughey spinning around in apparent confusion as he also stands upright. The camera tilts up to keep them in frame, and it moves with Freeman to make the move seem natural while adding a sense of speed to the scene.

As your actors move, reframe to keep them in shot, but tilt the camera at the same speed as one of the actors.

McConaughey stumbles forward, almost hesitating between Freeman and the table, but in case we are in any doubt about his fury and frustration, he grabs the table and upends it.

When a character is frustrated, show a physical reaction to the frustration, and if possible show another reaction before the cut.

This scene opens with horses dragging a carriage toward camera. This could be the beginning of a journey, but as the horses approach the camera, we pan with them and tilt down to see their feet coming to a stop in the dust.

When you're telling a story at speed, cut out every detail you can. If there's a journey, show only its final moments.

After a brief wide shot of the carriage outside the house, we cut to a distorted reflection of the house in the carriage window. Despite the pace of this scene, it shouldn't feel rushed. Freeman is concerned about the success of his mission, so a sense of pause is required. By focusing on the reflection, and then pulling focus to his anxious face, we get the feeling of a lengthy pause even though it only takes three seconds of screen time.

In the middle of apparent chaos, Spielberg shows us a calm, domestic image. This close-up of the watering can is brief, and we follow the spout as it is pulled away, leading the camera to the face of Anthony Hopkins. This is the moment that we realize he could be the potential solution to the problem. Despite his stern appearance, we remember seeing him earlier in the film, and sense that he may be able to help. This is one reason why this part of the film moves so rapidly. We could have watched the characters discuss a meeting with him, journey over, and debate the plan's potential success, but it's more effective when the audience gets a sudden jolt of hope by seeing this familiar face.

Start with a close-up of an object, then follow that object until it reveals a face that helps to tell your story. A revelation like this is a satisfying way to close a rapid sequence of images.

As Hopkins begins to talk we cut to the wide shot, shot from a high camera angle. Being high up, we are able to see that Freeman is already present and that the discussion is underway. The two men are on opposite sides of the frame, showing a barrier that currently lies between them, but this brief story has been told. Disaster struck, a journey occurred, and help may now be at hand.

A wide shot can close your rapid story by showing that your character has reached the destination and is already making progress toward a solution.

CHAPTER 10

VISUAL STORYTELLING:
Empire of the Sun

SOME OF THE MOST ENJOYABLE sequences in Spielberg films occur when we are treated to a visual story. In this sequence, we see Christian Bale showing that he is no longer the aimless boy from earlier in the film. He charges from place to place, balancing his need to trade with generosity and friendship.

For this to work, Spielberg needs to show Bale making many successful trades to prove that Bale now lives this way. The sequence moves at a great pace, with Bale running, or being eager to run, throughout. Despite this, the repetition of these moments could become dull without strong visuals, so Spielberg uses all his best tricks to introduce complexity, humor, and contrast.

The opening shot, of dry soil being turned around withered cabbages, gives no hint about what is to come, but the image of the cabbage is vital later in the scene — so it's important we see it now.

In fast-moving sequences, use an image in your opening frame that returns later in the sequence to help the audience keep track of what's going on in the story.

The camera tilts up the body of the gardener, and we assume we're watching him until we see Bale running in from the left of frame. We pan with him until he taps the gardener, offering up the cigarettes. Having him cross behind the gardener creates more visual interest than if he had run up to the space in the left of frame.

Shoot your actor entering the scene at speed, and pan with them to establish that when the character stops it is only a brief pause, and that more action will follow.

An extreme close-up on the exchange of goods is important early in the sequence. We now know that any time he deals with people, he will be trading goods. When we cut back to the wide, we see the green cabbage being handed over to him. This flash of green shows up brightly against the sandy surroundings, making it a strong visual reference for several following parts of the sequence.

Use colorful objects to guide the audience's attention, especially when that object will recur several times during the scene.

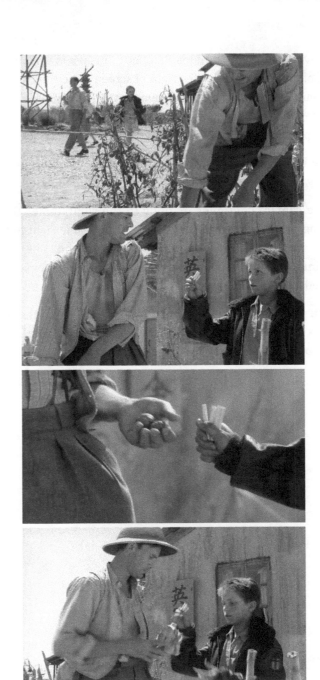

This wide shot almost hides Bale, but our eye is drawn to the flash of green cabbage on the right of screen as he runs to the left of frame. When he sets off, the camera dollies to the right while panning with him, bringing him to the center of frame and making his approach seem extremely rapid.

Dolly in the opposite direction of a distant actor, and pan slowly, to create a sense of speed through the location.

As the camera continues its dolly to the right, James Greene, playing golf in the foreground, passes from frame right to frame left, with Bale approaching in the background. The camera continues to dolly right and pan left so that Bale is eventually framed between the two adults.

When you've set up a dolly move, let it continue so that other actors come into frame. This helps create depth, making the location feel like a real and populated place.

The camera has stopped, and Bale rushes out to the right of frame, causing Greene to turn around and watch him flee. Greene walks toward the center of frame, and the camera dollies to the right as he does so we can see two adults watching Bale run. This introduces the idea that the adults are all aware of Bale and his exploits.

Using the same dolly track you set up earlier, block your actors so that the dolly can continue, again showing us a new perspective on the location.

The dolly continues its move to the right, bringing Leslie Phillips — also watching Bale run through the camp — into an unexpected close-up. By having Phillips appear in the frame so unexpectedly, we are drawn into his amused fascination.

Place one actor close to the dolly track, but out of frame, so that the same dolly move eventually brings the character into a close-up.

The wide shot, taken from overhead, shows Bale moving fast through his surroundings. Everybody else is moving slowly, and most are going in the opposite direction. The camera moves down and pans with Bale, indicating that his is rising above the restrictions of his circumstances while also giving us a glimpse of the camp's scale.

When your actor runs through a wide shot, have everybody else move slowly in the other direction to create a stronger sense of character motion.

The camera now dollies alongside Bale at speed, using a long lens to exaggerate the sense of motion through the crowd. As the dolly slows, he too slows and heads away from the camera. The camera comes to a stop and heads around obstacles, crossing back toward the left of frame. This change of direction underlines the feeling of speeding through obstacles more than if he simply ran away from the camera.

Dolly with your actor, and when the camera stops have the actor move across frame in the opposite direction so that we can see the character speeding through the location.

As Bale runs in from the left of frame, we can see that he is holding half of the green cabbage. This brief flash of color is all we need to see to know that a trade will take place. When he reaches the right of frame he immediately changes direction, heading to the left of frame, and the camera pans with him until he is obscured by the laundry. This scene takes place largely behind the laundry, with only glimpses of Bale and the children as the laundry flutters upward.

Once you've established a pattern, you can keep the scene interesting by using lots of direction changes, and even obscuring the action behind foreground objects. This works best when the objects are in motion, giving us a few glimpses of what's happening.

The camera pans right as Bale heads off that way, and, once again, he changes direction, moving off to the left. The continual changes of direction create a strong sense of urgency.

Without ever cutting, you can create the sensation of speed by panning one way to follow the actor, and then having the actor lurch in the other direction.

This shot begins with the children's makeshift go-karts heading down the ramp from right to left. A moment later, Spielberg has Bale rush in from the left. His appearance is more dramatic because he is running in the opposite direction of the motion in the background.

Set up action in the background, and then have your main character run in the opposite direction of that motion. Keep the actor close to camera, and whip-pan to enhance the sense of a sudden arrival.

The camera whip-pans and immediately dollies toward him as he approaches the woman at the table. We continue to dolly in as he places the bright green cabbage on the table, and we close in on that cabbage as the woman covers it with her hat. This sequence is only half done at this point, but Spielberg continues to find original ways to convey Bale's brief but rapid adventure through the camp.

After a rapid pan, have the actor move away from the camera, and then dolly in toward the action. This gives us the feeling that we're trying to catch up with the action.

CONCLUSION

My hope is that, having read this book, you will have seen how the simplest of camera moves can lead to the deepest emotions. When you add these skills to your arsenal, you will be a better filmmaker without ever having to copy Spielberg.

When you have studied the films covered in the book, you should also watch classics, such as *The Color Purple*, to see how the same ideas can be used to create different results. Even in films as varied as *The Terminal*, *Munich*, and *War Horse*, you will see the huge range of emotions and effects that these techniques create.

One area that has not been covered in this book, because it has been covered so extensively in the three *Master Shots* books, is Spielberg's use of reflections. If you want to see how reflections can be used to show two things at once, or introduce new information, watch *A.I. Artificial Intelligence* and *Minority Report*, and then study the *Master Shots* books. Spielberg went through a stage where he was obsessed with reflections, and he makes masterful use of this device.

The greatest challenge you will find when working with Spielberg's techniques is getting the actors to cooperate with your choices. Some actors will say that the blocking is too restrictive, and others will even want to improvise rather than hit exact marks. Actors often panic because they worry that you are more concerned about the camerawork than their performance. It might help to show them this book so they know what you are trying to achieve. Watch Ralph Fiennes in *Schindler's List* and you will see that no matter how exact the blocking, he was able to create a mesmerizing performance. Reassure your actors that these techniques will enhance their performance so it can be seen more clearly and more dramatically than when shot in a standard way.

It's important to create your own style, but when you use the techniques shown in this book, you can enhance your skills and make better films than you've ever made before.

ABOUT THE AUTHOR

Christopher Kenworthy worked as a writer, director, and producer for fourteen years. He directed a feature film, along with many music videos and commercial projects. Currently he is focused on writing.

Christopher is the author of the bestselling *Master Shots Vol 1*, *Master Shots Vol 2*, and *Master Shots Vol 3: The Director's Vision*. He is also the author of two novels and many short stories.

Born in England, he lives in Australia with two daughters and the actor Molly Kerr.

www.christopherkenworthy.com

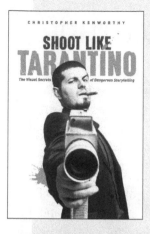

SHOOT LIKE TARANTINO
The Visual Secrets of Dangerous Directing

Christopher Kenworthy

Want your film to sizzle with danger? Then learn from the master of tension and action. Using Tarantino's secret tricks for creating conflict, keeping dialogue taut, and letting all hell break loose, you will enhance your own shooting style. Whatever your budget, get the action pumping with the camera setups and moves revealed in this dynamic book.

$15.95 · 144 PAGES · ORDER #217RLS · ISBN 9781615932252

SHOOT LIKE SCORSESE:
The Visual Secrets of Shock, Elegance, and Extreme Character

Christopher Kenworthy

Without the right camera moves, an actor's performance is hidden. Scorsese is a great storyteller, but his greatest skill is telling a visual story that makes room for the actor's performance. This means that whatever actors you are working with, you can use the Scorsese techniques to make every performance shine, whether you're shooting subtle romance or tense confrontations.

$15.95 · 144 PAGES · ORDER #SCORSESE · ISBN 9781615932320

CHRISTOPHER KENWORTHY worked as a writer, director, and producer for fourteen years. He directed a feature film, along with many music videos and commercial projects. Currently he is focused on writing.

Christopher is the author of the internationally bestselling *Master Shots* series (three volumes). He also shot, wrote, and created the groundbreaking *Master Shots* eBook series, available on the Apple iBook platform. www.mwp.com

Born in England, he currently lives in Australia with two daughters and the actor Molly Kerr.

{ THE MYTH OF MWP }

In a dark time, a light bringer came along, leading the curious and the frustrated to clarity and empowerment. It took the well-guarded secrets out of the hands of the few and made them available to all. It spread a spirit of openness and creative freedom, and built a storehouse of knowledge dedicated to the betterment of the arts.

The essence of the Michael Wiese Productions (MWP) is empowering people who have the burning desire to express themselves creatively. We help them realize their dreams by putting the tools in their hands. We demystify the sometimes secretive worlds of screenwriting, directing, acting, producing, film financing, and other media crafts.

By doing so, we hope to bring forth a realization of 'conscious media' which we define as being positively charged, emphasizing hope and affirming positive values like trust, cooperation, self-empowerment, freedom, and love. Grounded in the deep roots of myth, it aims to be healing both for those who make the art and those who encounter it. It hopes to be transformative for people, opening doors to new possibilities and pulling back veils to reveal hidden worlds.

MWP has built a storehouse of knowledge unequaled in the world, for no other publisher has so many titles on the media arts. Please visit www.mwp.com where you will find many free resources and a 25% discount on our books. Sign up and become part of the wider creative community!

Onward and upward,

Michael Wiese
Publisher/Filmmaker